Going Through The

Storms of Life

RODERICK AGUILLARD

FIRST EDITION

ISBN: 978-1-936989-52-2

Library of Congress Control Number: 2012932445

Published by
NewBookPublishing.com,
a division of Reliance Media, Inc.
2395 Apopka Blvd., #200, Apopka, FL 32703
NewBookPublishing.com

Printed in the United States of America

Dedicated
to the life of
Lynne Aguillard Venus

11-12-1964 to 12-11-2008

I still recall the birth of my lovely daughter, Lynne. She was born on a wintery day in November 1964. At her birth, I was not a born-again believer. However, this beautiful gift from God caused me to re-evaluate the wickedness of my life and she became the beginning of a godly change.

During her fourth year of life, I encountered the Lord

Jesus and I began to raise my children in the faith. Lynne was always a sweetheart, my most spiritual child, loving Jesus throughout her teenage life and marrying a godly man at the young age of 19.

At the age of 22, a generational curse called bi-polar disorder took over her mind and we basically lost her to this mental oppression for 22 years. She was in and out of mental wards. We fought the good fight of faith, but lost her to a tragic suicide on December 11, 2008. Out of this suffering, much of this book has been born. To her wonderful and loving heart, I dedicate this book that, I pray, will touch and change the lives of thousands.

Lynne,
I love you and sorely miss you.
I will see you on the other side.
Daddy

Table of Contents

Foreword

Bro. Rod Aguillard has been a spiritual father in my life for the past 11 years. It was from this relationship, and through sharing my own struggles overcoming mental illness, that I became acquainted with his daughter, Lynne.

Lynne and I did not grow up together. We did not develop a close friendship over years of laughter and sharing time with our families. No, our kinship was an understanding of the ravaging depths to which you are plunged in the battle for your mind. For more than a decade, I only heard from Lynne during such dark times. But, we shared an understanding of one another that made us instantly comfortable, and immediately and intimately close.

The fall of 2008 was one of those seasons. Lynne had moved home with her parents, and I was working as an assistant for Bro. Rod and his son, Pastor Stephen Aguillard.

Lynne spent hours every day sitting in my office over a period of several months. We cried and prayed as she desperately sought freedom. Lynne wanted more than anything to rebuild her life and be the tremendous woman whom we all saw clearly she was created to be. There was much counseling and encouragement – and I believed with everything in me, without one shadow of a doubt – that she would be delivered, to be a living testimony of the great glory of God. I never once considered a different outcome. I never in all of my years faced a storm like the one brewing.

And, I'll probably never understand, this side of heaven, why things ended the way they did that December day.

Suicide is something so dark and shocking and incomprehensible. It changes everything. Honestly, one of my first thoughts when Mrs. Mary told me the news was, "Oh, dear God, Bro. Rod will never be the same." That was an understatement. Who knew how God would turn the tide? Who knew that He would use Lynne to show His great glory through such a great tragedy? I have learned much watching Bro. Rod and Mrs. Mary navigate through the waters of this unimaginable storm. One of the greatest lessons they have taught me is how to suffer well. I am thankful to them for opening their lives in such a transparent way so that others might be touched, even edified, through the things they have endured. Bro. Rod shares their experiences beautifully in this book; how, with Jesus, no tear is ever wasted, no pain is too great for grace, and no matter the darkness of the hour, joy really does come in the morning.

Laurie Ray

Sister in Christ, Church Secretary

Chapter One

The Storm And
The Deliverer

The ultimate revelation of the Godhead is the Father. The Holy Spirit has come to reveal Jesus. Jesus came to reveal the Father. The Lord's Prayer is all about the Father. He starts off the model prayer by stating, "Our Father in heaven, hallowed be Your name. Your kingdom come, the Father's kingdom. Your will be done on earth, the Father's will. Give us this day our daily bread. Father forgive us."- Matthew 6:9-12. He told Philip, "If you see me, you see the Father."-John 14:9.

In Exodus 3:7-8, we see the Father's heart for His children. The Lord said, "I have seen the oppression of my people, I heard their cry. I know their sorrows." We serve a Father who sees, and who hears and knows our sorrows and setbacks. The writer concludes that we serve a God who comes down to deliver us out of the hand of our enemy, and delivers us into a good land, one flowing with milk and honey. Our Lord delivers us from the land of drugs and drinks, of setbacks and sorrows, of difficulties and disappointments into a land of peace and prosperity. He delivers us into a land of purity and power. We serve a deliverer! [1]Declares God, "When the enemy comes in like a flood, the spirit of the Lord will lift up a standard against him and the Deliverer (Jesus) shall come to Zion."-Isaiah 59:19-20. Glory to God, we serve a great deliverer, a supernatural someone who comes to liberate; a redeemer who comes to set us free. A deliverer is someone who rescues us from the storms and setbacks of life. The angel told Joseph that Mary would bear a Son and said, "You shall call Him Jesus (Savior) for He will deliver His people from their sins."-Matthew 1:21. Thank God we serve a deliverer who sets us free from our sins and rescues us from the storms of life!

The psalmist declared "Many are the afflictions of the righteous."-Psalms 34:19. Many are the problems and pressures; many are the setbacks and heartbreaks; and many are the difficulties and disappointments of God's children. I heard it said that there are four cycles in our life: we are either going into a storm; in the midst of a storm; coming out of a storm; or in a season of fair weather. My wife and I have been through several major storms but I am grateful that our skies are clearing.

Let us consider the storms of life and our deliverer. Keep a copy of this book because one day, perhaps, you will need words of wisdom and encouragement as you go through the storms of life.

Chapter Two

Seven Words Of
Storm Wisdom

"There arose a great storm."-Mark 4:37. You have heard the saying, "Out of the blue, this storm or squall came on me." This was a common happening on the Sea of Galilee. The Sea of Galilee is about 13 miles long and 7 miles wide, and 702 feet below sea level. The small sea is surrounded by mountains. At unexpected times, the cool air will come down from the mountains and flow into the warm air over the Sea of Galilee. Then suddenly, out of seemingly nowhere, a violent wind storm can occur. The Scripture said, "There arose a <u>great storm</u>," a mega-storm which denotes something of magnificent proportions, not a mere rainstorm, but a storm of turbulent or violent wind.

So it is in our life. One day we are in fair weather, then, suddenly, out of nowhere, we find ourselves in a storm of life. On December 11, 2008, Mary and I were actually in hope of our oldest daughter's recovery. Lynne Aguillard Venus had been suffering from a bi-polar mental oppression for 22 years. She was divorced, living in a cottage behind our main house. For four months, Mary and I and others had ministered to her in bringing her out of a deep state of depression. During this week of December, our hopes were high as she seemed to be coming out of the depression. As a hairdresser, she was back to work and on this 11th day of December, she had completed three hair appointments, and people at the salon said she was smiling and seemingly at peace. Around noon, Lynne took her three-year-old son to Angelle, my youngest daughter to babysit. On her way back to the salon for another hair appointment, something must have snapped in her mind. Mary and I arrived at our home at about 2 p.m. on a snowy day in southeast Louisiana. As Mary walked in, she found a note on our kitchen counter, "Jesus, please forgive me, I love all of you." Mary cried out to me, "Rod, Lynne has hurt herself!" I ran to the cottage, but she was not there. Then, I knew where she was – in my bedroom. As I walked into the bedroom, Lynne was lying on the floor in a pool of blood. She had found my pistol and taken her life. On that tragic day, we encountered the most horrific storm of our earthly lives. We met a lion in a pit on a snowy day. The storm that you are in or will be in may not be as violent, but my hope is that our experience of going through the storms of life will encourage and strengthen you. The following are seven words of storm wisdom to see you through the setbacks and sufferings of life.

First Word Of Storm Wisdom:
Storms Are Certain

Just because you are in the midst of an overwhelming storm doesn't mean you are in sin or out of the will of God. Just the opposite may be true. In your suffering and setbacks, you are probably in the center of His will, even closer to the Man of Sorrows.

Jesus promised, "In the world, you shall have tribulations, trials and tears, but be of good cheer. Be confident, for I have overcome the world. I have deprived it of its power to conquer you."-John 16:33. This promise of victory is shouting grounds. See it, seize it, and say it. Your victory through the storms of life is certain. The Psalmist declared, "Many are the afflictions of the righteous." Many are the problems and pressures; the difficulties and disappointments; the setbacks and heartbreaks of the righteous. "BUT!" As someone said, thank God for the Holy "buts" of the Bible. "But the Lord delivers us from them all."-Psalms 34:19. As I write this, I predict that your skies will be clearing as you read these words of storm wisdom.

I have a personal storm list with which you might identify. There are financial storms, and Mary and I have been through a few of these in our church setbacks. On two occasions, there was no money for our salary. There are marital storms. Early on, we had our share of this. Twenty years ago, Mary learned the words "adapt to your husband." It has been smooth sailing since that revelation (smiling!) There are physical storms, mental storms of fear and worry, and storms of a wayward child. There is the storm of a child's tragic death. We have been through enough storms to sink two or three Titanics, but we are still standing, still serving, and still shouting. His indescribable grace or strength is sufficient.

Second Word Of Storm Wisdom: God Is

I read this on Facebook. Someone quoted a church sign that stated two great truths: 1. There is a God. 2. You are not He. God is. Hebrews 11:6 declares, "Without faith, it is impossible to please God. He that comes to God must believe that He is. God is." The moon, the stars and the heavens declare that God is. The fiery red maples of an autumn in New England declare that God is. The beautiful soft snowflakes of the frozen Yankee north declare that God is. The druggies and the drunkards and the nobodies being saved declare that God is.

In 1968, yours truly had no merit or morals. On an April night, I was in a go-go joint. I left at 5 a.m., intoxicated. That afternoon, my wife left me with our two children. I was hung over with my family and finances broken, with my body being broken over the pleasures of sin. In this state of a sin crisis, the Holy Spirit convicted me of my lost and broken state. Lying in the bathtub, I prayed a sinner's prayer, "Lord help me." In my surrender and repentance, I was born again. My new life of joy, peace, and righteousness declares that God is. My wife and children can testify and declare that God is.

I want to say it again, God is. Through the good times, the bad times, the glad times and the sad times, the righteous declare that God is. Going through a marsh storm in southeast Louisiana, I can declare that God is. A week after our daughter's funeral, my son, who is a pastor, said, "Dad let me take you duck hunting on our lease in the sweetwater marshes of southeast Louisiana." I resisted because I didn't want to leave my wife Mary. She was in a deep struggle with our daughter's tragic death. She encouraged me to get out of the house and air out in the great outdoors. As we sat in our blinded boat in the marsh, a dense Louisiana fog set in. We couldn't see but a few yards in the distance. Sitting in the dense fog, my middle daughter Amber called me and said, "Dad you need to come home. Mama is not doing well." That concerned me because I deeply love and cherish my wife. Then, a second call came from Pastor Mike Boudreaux, who is like a son to me, and who is a pastor I sent to oversee and shepherd a church near Kansas City. He said, "Brother Rod you need to go home and see about your wife." At that point, I told Stephen, "Let's crank it up; I need to get home to your mother." We tried to find our way to Lake Leary. We knew if we could find the lake, finding the way home was easy because even in a dense fog, we could follow the shoreline to a canal and then to the landing. In a matter of a few minutes, in the marsh storm fog, we found ourselves going in circles. Finally, I told Stephen to shut the engine down. I called my secretary and asked her to call a few intercessors for a breakthrough to get home. As we sat, we heard human voices in front of us. I stood and shouted for help. The voices stopped. We drove in that direction and stopped again. Then, the human voices of men came again right in front of us. I stood up and shouted for help again. The voices stopped. Stephen drove toward the voices in our mud boat and stopped. Then he said, "Dad, I think I see a break in the marsh; it could be the lake." As we went for the break, somewhere near the voices, we rode into Lake Leary on our way home to my lovely wife. At the truck, Stephen said, "Dad, there were no men there. Do you think it was angels?" I affirmed, it was angels assigned to minister to the heirs of salvation. God is.

Not only is God is, but God is with you. Isaiah saw it, "When you pass through the waters, I will be with you. When you go through the rivers, they will not overflow you. When you walk through the fire, it will not burn you."-Isaiah 43:12. Why? Because God is, and God is with you. Also, Christ is in you and God is for you! Since God is for you who in hell or in this world can be against you? He is our present help in the time of storms or troubles. He said, "Call upon me in the day of trouble (the day of your personal storm) and I will deliver you, and you shall glorify me."-Psalms 50:15. Storms and sufferings don't bring glory to God; rather your deliverance in the midst of it brings glory to God. God Himself delivers you because He delights in you. Let's rejoice!

Third Word Of Storm Wisdom:
He Is The Master Of The Storm

"There arose a great storm, but He was in the stern, asleep on a pillow."-Mark 4:37-38 "What was a tomb to the disciples was a cradle to Jesus," Max Lucado wrote. How could He sleep in the midst of danger and death? It's simple: He was and is in charge of the storm. Jesus has dominion. He has all authority in Heaven and in the earth. He rules. The devil doesn't rule. You and I are in His hands, not the devil's hands. If we were in the devil's hands, we all would be dead by morning. Jesus Christ is Lord! He has the last word on every personal storm. Shout!

The writer of Ephesians declares that God rules. He is the master of your storm! "God raised Him from the dead and set Him on a throne in deep Heaven. He is in charge of running the universe, everything from galaxies to governments. No name and no power is exempt from His rule. And not just for the time being, but for forever."-Ephesians 1:20-22 (The Message). He is in charge of it all and has the final word on everything, every setback and every storm in your life.

Let's rejoice that God is in charge of it all. Nothing in your life or in my life takes Him by surprise. He permits the storm and He superintends the storm. Read this scenario in Job's mega-storm. He lost his wealth, his children and, eventually, His health. He went through a hell storm but God is. God had the last word; He restored what the devil had stolen. In God's restoration, there is always divine compensation: He restored two-fold of everything that Job had lost. Job's latter end was greater than his former. Again, God had the last word. Let me encourage you in the grace of our Lord Jesus: He will have the last word on your financial setback, and He will have the last word on your marital conflict. He will have the last word on your wayward child. He will have the last word on your physical setback. Whatever your personal storm may be, He will have the last word, but only if you trust Him! Refuse to charge God in the midst of your storm. Rather, do as Job did: Bless Him, Praise Him and declare, "Though He slay me, yet I will trust Him."-Job 13:15.

Fourth Word Of Storm Wisdom:
It Is Normal To Question God

It is normal to question God. "And a great windstorm arose. They awoke Jesus and said, 'Teacher, do you not care that we are perishing?'-Mark 4:37-38. The normal initial response in the midst of a crisis or a major setback is to question God. Don't you care about my marriage? About my children? About my finances? About my future? My boat is being swamped and I am about to go under! What's happening? Have I sinned? What have I done wrong? Where is God?

For a season, it is OK to ask God why. You just can't stay there or you will move into a spirit of doubt, discouragement, and unbelief. In the midst of your initial questioning, don't charge God. Again, Job lost his children and his wealth and the scripture reports, "in all this Job did not sin nor charge God with wrong."-Job 1:22. Job held fast to his integrity and his faithfulness to bless and trust God through it all.

I have served the Lord for more than 44 years. I have been through some horrific storms, setbacks and heartbreaks. Through it all, I have never once charged God. In the midst of the storm, I have questioned God. I have asked Him why. Father, where are you? What's happening?

Several years ago, when Amy Stockstill died, thousands of us who loved her fasted and prayed. We believed for a breakthrough, a healing of cancer. She was so young, in her mid-20s, vivacious and making an impact on thousands of young people. She was married to a maturing prophet, Joel

Stockstill, and they were a mighty duo for the Kingdom of God. But, in less than a year, the cancer took her life much to our dismay and grief. Following her funeral, I wrote God a letter asking Him why. I reminded Him of all the promises of the tens of thousands of people who stood in the gap. Also, I remind Him of some prophetic words that indicated a healing, yet she died in the flower of her youth. Why, God, I asked? Several weeks later an answer came, "It's none of your business." Case closed. Perhaps she was a casualty of war. It is obvious to me that in our war with the darkness, we will lose some to premature death. Also, through our setbacks and heartbreaks, the Holy Spirit is using them as death blows to our self-will to bring about brokenness and a deeper flow of the anointing.

On July 4, 2004, Reserve Christian Church, the church I pastored for 37 years had a picnic celebration. I left early just to come home and relax, as, I am not much on picnics. I was not really seeking the Lord, but suddenly in the backroom of my home, the Holy Spirit visited me. In the visitation, I began to weep, and *rhemas* began to come into my heart. First, He said "I am going to use you in spite of your sins and shortcomings." That was an exciting and encouraging word, as I still fall short on occasions. Secondly, He said, "I am going to baptize you with a baptism of fire out of which you will preach a word of repentance to the body, a trumpet for consecration." Thirdly, He said, "I am going to separate you from all that is carnal, secular, and sensual." At that point, I was thanking Him for sanctification, that He was separating me into the Father's heart that none should perish! Finally, He said, "I am going to break you into a thousand pieces and pour you out on the Body of Christ!" In the storm of the tragic death of my oldest daughter, lovely Lynne, He broke me into a thousand pieces. I cried a river! She was a casualty of war.

Presently, God is avenging me of all I suffered. He has broken me into a thousand pieces and is now pouring me out upon the body with a message of hope: His grace is sufficient and what the enemy means for destruction, God will turn into our edification. There may be weeping for the night, but joy will come in the morning. God is faithful. Joy has come and the body is being encouraged by the power of His anointing flowing through broken vessels. To God be the Glory!

Fifth Word Of Storm Wisdom:
Face Your Storm

I am going to express this word of wisdom through the parable of three birds. See this parable in the eye of your imagination.

The first bird: When a storm approaches, an ostrich puts his head in the ground hoping it will simply pass without harm. As the windstorm picks up in velocity, he remains with his head buried in the sand. At some point, in the crisis of the storm, the wind picks him up by his buttocks and throws him over with a flip, breaking his neck in half. Don't be an ostrich and bury your head, hoping the storm will pass.

The second bird: When the storm approaches, a chicken begins to fear and starts cackling. At some point, as the winds increase, she turns her back to the wind, flaps her wings and begins to cackle like she was laying eggs. The force of the wind picks her up by her buttocks and drives her into the chicken wire, breaking her neck. Foolish chicken, she refused to face the storm.

The third bird: When the eagle sees a storm approaching, he flies to the cleft of the rock. As an eagle, he sits boldly facing the storm. No cackling, no head in the sand. He perches comfortably with a determined eye looking directly into the darkness and winds of the storm. As the winds begin to pick up with great force, he dives into the raging winds and mounts his wings. As he mounts his wings, at a precise moment of time, he begins soaring over the storm. What came to destroy him now elevates him. In his victory over the storm, he cries with an eagle's cry of victory. "Glory!" "Victory!"

Don't be an ostrich; don't ignore your storm. Don't be a chicken and turn your back to the storm with cackles of complaints and by saying poor me. Rather, be an eagle, face your storm and by the grace of God, dive into the winds that have come to destroy and you will fulfill, "Those who wait upon the Lord, shall mount up wings like eagles. They shall run and not be weary, they shall walk and not faint."-Isaiah 40:31. Glory to God! Declare to Him that you are an eagle! Face your storm!

Sixth Word Of Storm Wisdom:
There Is An End

"Then He arose and rebuked the wind and said to the sea, 'Peace, be still!' And the wind ceased and there was a great (mega) calm."-Matthew 8:26. There was an end to the storm over the Sea of Galilee. Another translation states, 'Awake now', He said to the sea, 'Quiet, settle down!' The wind ran out of breath, the sea became smooth as glass." (The Message)

The great good news in every storm is that there is an end. My oldest daughter had her first mental breakdown on Christmas Eve of 1987. Her husband and I had to admit her into a mental health facility in Hattiesburg, Mississippi. It was one of the most heartbreaking nights of my life. As the darkness of the storm hovered over us, a young man in the church gave me a word in season at the end of a Sunday morning church service. I had walked with him through a mental breakdown of a family member that had lasted for several months. I remember him bringing them to my office often during the week to lay hands on her head rebuking the mental oppression. He faced his storm and eventually she was delivered. He came to me that Sunday morning and said, "Bro. Rod, I don't understand it all, but there is an end!

May I encourage you in the midst of your storm, now or whenever it comes, there is an end! Your weeping will turn into joy. Your bitter moments will turn into sweetness. Your day of adversity will move into a day of prosperity. It may be Friday, but Sunday is coming. It is a truth: Your personal storm will have an ending and the skies will clear.

Again, Job was tested for a season in the storm of his earthly life. He was tested until faith was borne. "Though he slay me, yet I will trust Him."-Job 13:15. Because he faced his storm with the grace of God, the storm had a good ending. "The Lord restored his fortunes and gave him (Job) twice as much as he had before. The Lord blessed the latter days of Job more than his beginning."-Job 42:10, 12. Yes indeed, storms faced with the grace of God will have a good ending.

The following is an excerpt from "The Storm" from *Streams in the Desert* by L.B. Cowman: "The storm came and there was devastation! It uprooted strong oaks and blew away the spider webs. But, soon, the lightning was gone. The thunder ceased and was silent, and the rain was over. Then there arose a sweet, gentle western wind that chased away the dark, ominous clouds. Then, I saw the retreating storm throw a scarf of rainbows over her fair shoulders and glowing neck. She looked back at me and smiled and passed from my sight. Many weeks after the storm, the fields raised their hands full of flagrant flowers toward the sky, and all summer, the grass was greener, the streams were full and flowing, and the trees with lush foliage cast a restful shade. All this was because the storm had come. All this was as though the earth had forgotten the darkened skies and the howling winds of the storm."

Seventh Word Of Storm Wisdom:
The Power Of The Prayer
Of Agreement And Praise

"Again I say to you that if two of you agree on earth

concerning anything that they ask, it will be done for them by My Father in heaven."-Matthew 18:19. Don't be foolish: Face your storm. Be a realist and don't be an ostrich, denying the winds that have come to divide and destroy you. Over the 42 years of serving our Lord, I have watched individuals who deny the symptoms of sickness, mental oppressions, marital conflicts, financial setbacks, etc. They keep it a secret from the body, thinking that others will make bad confessions or pray negatively. In your storm, don't run from the body of believers, run to the body. There is much grace and power in the prayer of agreement. I recently shared with a believer who was going through a major physical attack, "Don't deny the reality of the sickness. Seek the reality of the Healer!" Face your storm! Get people of faith involved in your storm with the prayer of agreement for a breakthrough whether it's a mental storm, marital storm, financial storm, physical storm, storm of a wayward child, or addiction storm. Cry out to the Lord in your troubles and get others to cry out with you. Together, we win. It's not a "me" deal or a "secret" deal, it's a "we "deal!

God loves for people to praise Him in the midst of a storm. God inhabits the praise of His people. He is attracted to a thankful heart in the midst of a crisis or a setback. My former daughter-in-law went through a major storm in her divorce with my oldest son and in the custody of her three sons and daughter. It was a nightmare for all of us, but we faced the storm. She wrote this thought to me in the midst of the storm winds that came to divide and destroy: "Just as there is calm in the eye of 'hurricane,' so is Jesus in the midst of our storm. Without my hope in Him and the knowledge of Scripture, I would have never been able to find that peace. I became a prisoner of hope, always reminding God of His Word. "For as the rain comes down, and the snow from heaven, And do not return there, But water the earth,And make it bring forth and bud, That it may give seed to the sower, And bread to the eater, So shall My word be that goes forth from My mouth; It shall not return to Me void, But it shall accomplish what I please, And it shall prosper *in the thing* for which I sent it."-Isaiah 55:10-11 (NKJV). Every dream, every promise is worth the storm. If we stay in faith, God will bring us out of the storm. The voice of victory is found in God's Word. There is something wonderfully attractive about the storm, but there's also something frightening about it, too. It is dangerously unpredictable. A storm can turn an angelic sky (my seemingly happy marriage and family) into the devil's cauldron. There's a tension between beauty and danger. There are things to be seen, heard, and experienced nowhere else. It has been an awareness of danger, but at the same moment, an alertness to the reality of God. The storm has taught me that there is beauty everywhere. I have learned to see God in places and things that I would have never previously thought to look. Just as David did, in God, I have learned to take my refuge, praying, and believing, wide-eyed, waiting for God to make good to His Word. I have learned that praising and believing God through the storm have been my greatest witnesses to the lost world around me. I cannot begin to tell you how many opportunities I have been given to share my faith with others, not because of a rehearsed salvation message, but simply through my keeping my faith in God, knowing and believing that even this storm is going to work out to my good. It has and it will. I still believe God for the restoration of my family. I will never stop."

Again, as stated earlier, Ephesians declares that God is the master of your storm! "All this energy issues from Christ: God raised him from death and set him on a throne in deep heaven, in charge of running the universe, everything from galaxies to governments, no name and no power exempt from His rule. And not just for the time being, but forever. He is in charge of it all, has the final word on everything. At the center of all this, Christ rules the church." The church, you see, is not peripheral to the world; the world is peripheral to the church. The church is Christ's body, in which He speaks and acts, by which He fills everything with His presence."- Ephesians 1:20-21 (The Message). Let's rejoice that God is in charge of it all. Nothing in your life or in my life takes Him by surprise. He permits the storm and He superintends the storm. Again, God had the last word. Let me encourage you in the grace of our Lord. He will have the last word on your financial setback, He will have the last word on your marital conflict. He will have the last word on your wayward child. He will have the last word on your physical setback. Whatever, your personal storm may be, He will have the last word, but only if you trust Him! Refuse to charge God in the midst of your storm, but rather bless Him and declare to your enemy that God rules. The outcome of your storm will have a good ending. Victorious overcoming is certain.

Chapter Three

Seven Positive Results Of Going Through Storms

I remind you that the storms, setbacks, and sufferings of life are certain. We live in enemy territory. This is not Heaven. Pastor Mike Mille' said, "For the believers, our earthly journey is as close to hell as we will ever get. For the unbeliever, this early journey is as close to Heaven as he will ever get." I choose to walk with Jesus through the storms and setbacks of life.

There are two truths of Scripture on the certainty of personal storms.

1. We have been chosen in the furnace of affliction. "Behold, I have refined thee, but not with silver; I have chosen thee in the furnace of affliction."-Isaiah 48:10. We have

been chosen in the furnace of pressures and problems; the furnace of difficulties and disappointments; and the furnace of setbacks and heartbreaks. I am so grateful that the devil doesn't have his hand on the temperature dial of our personal furnace. Rather, the Holy Spirit has his hand on our furnace and when He has purified us, we shall come forth as gold to the glory of our Heavenly Father.

2. The Holy Spirit promised us that we must go through much tribulation (trials and tears) to enter into the Kingdom of God.-Acts 14:22. In my 44 years of serving Him, I have experienced much joy and peace, but at the same time I have gone through much tribulation, trials, and tears. But, through it all, I have learned to trust Him. Through it all, He has been as a refiner's fire, purifying me until there was birthed a passion for Jesus and the souls of men. I am very grateful!

Here are the seven positive results of going through the storms of life.

First Positive Result Of The Storms Of Life:
The Storms And Sufferings
Of Life Produce Enlargement

"Hear me when I call, O God of my righteousness! You have relieved me in *my* distress; Have mercy on me, and hear my prayer."-Psalms 4:1. "Blessed *be* the God and Father of our Lord Jesus Christ, the Father of mercies and God of all comfort, who comforts us in all our tribulation, that we may be able to comfort those who are in any trouble, with the comfort with which we ourselves are comforted by God."-II Corinthians 1:3-4.

We serve the God of all comfort. The Holy Spirit is the Great Comforter. He is the one alongside us who strengthens us to walk through the setbacks of life. Much more, He is our inside Helper. When our human strength gives out, our inside strengthener kicks in. The night of our oldest daughter's tragic death, Mary and I laid in bed holding each other with tears and a broken heart. At one point, Mary said, "Rod, I believe my heart is going to burst!" As I held her, I cried out to the Great Comforter, "Help! Lord, help us!" Somehow, someway, His inside strength kicked in and we had grace to live through the night, the morrow, and the weeks and the months that followed. Now, with this same comfort, we can comfort others in the pain of their sufferings. It is our joy to help heal those who are brokenhearted and give them hope that a better day is coming. Over the past weeks, months, and years, our roots have gone deeper in the grace of God to strengthen others.

Second Positive Result Of The Storms Of Life:
Storms Separate Us

In every storm, the Holy Spirit is doing a deep work of sanctification or separating us into the Father's heart. In our suffering or setback, we bow low and are being conformed to the image or character of Jesus Christ. Hosea the prophet declared it, "In their affliction they will seek me early, earnestly."-Hosea 5:15. The writer of Ecclesiastes made it plain and simple, "Sorrow is better than laughter, for by the sadness of life, the heart is made better."-Ecclesiastes 7:3.

In much sorrow, there is laughter. Through it all, my heart has experienced the DNA of our Heavenly Father, which is joy unspeakable and full of glory! In the joy of the Lord, I express my faith or release His presence into the lives of others. In February 2011, I went to have an ultrasound on my heart as part of a check-up. A young lady was the technician doing the work on me. On that particular morning, I had been in His presence; the joy of His Kingdom was flowing through me, touching her life. Two weeks later, I went back for an ultrasound on my legs. As I walked into her lab, she said, "Before you take your clothes off, I need to share a testimony. When you walked in two weeks ago, if you have asked me my religion, I would have told you atheist. I knew you were a pastor, and I felt some kind of energy flowing through you. The good news, last week I got born again." To say the least, it made my day and still brings joy to my heart. In much sorrow, joy has come!

Third Positive Result Of The Storms Of Life: God's Power Increases In Us

"And he said unto me, My grace is sufficient for thee: for my strength is made perfect in weakness. Most gladly therefore will I rather glory in my infirmities, that the power of Christ may rest upon me. Therefore, I take pleasure in infirmities, in reproaches, in necessities, in persecutions, in distresses for Christ's sake: for when I am weak, then am I strong."-II Corinthians 12:9-10. As a child of God, you will never face a negative circumstance that exceeds His grace or strength. It is a truth: When you are weak, He is strong. When you are empty, He is full. I had a quickened word from Heaven right after my daughter's funeral, "He heals the broken hearted. He bandages their wounds."-Psalms 147:3. Mary and I took a shot to the gut on December 11, 2008, but through grace, God's power has done its deep work. I am convinced there is no trial that God's grace cannot match. As

Corrie ten Boom stated, "There is no pit so deep that Jesus is not deeper."

Fourth Positive Result Of The Storms Of Life:
Storms Prove Us And Equip Us For Service

"It is good for me that I have been afflicted; that I might learn thy statutes." -Psalms 119:71. The trials and storms of life equip us for service. In every storm or adverse circumstance, there are two hands at work. There is the hand of Satan that comes to discourage you, to divide you, and to destroy you. He comes to steal your faith and steal your praise through the storms and setbacks of life. He comes to cause you to question God, to charge Him and, eventually, give up on God. As Job's wife said, "Curse God and die!"-Job 2:9. Secondly, there is the hand of our Heavenly Father, that comes to sustain you and to strengthen you, to perfect your faith, and eventually equip you for service to set captives free and to comfort the afflicted.

Recently, I read the following in a devotional reading, "When God wants to make a servant, He puts him into the winds of a sudden storm. Yes, it is the storm that equips us for service. When God wants an oak tree, He plants it where the storms will shake it, and the rains will beat down upon it. It is in the midnight battle with the elements that the oak develops its rugged fiber and becomes the king of the Forest." *Streams in the Desert* –L.B. Cowman.

Since my oldest daughter's death, my roots have grown deep into the grace of God. The joy of the Lord has become my strength and I have a great capacity to love, to serve, to comfort, and to give hope. Glory to God!

Fifth Positive Result Of The Storms Of Life:
Storms Produce A Spirit Of Obedience

"Though he were a Son, yet learned he obedience by the things which he suffered."-Hebrews 5:8. Our Lord Jesus learned obedience through what he suffered. The prophet Isaiah saw it: "But he was wounded for our transgressions, he was bruised for our iniquities: the chastisement of our peace was upon him; and with his stripes we are healed. Yet it pleased the LORD to bruise him; he hath put him to grief: when thou shalt make his soul an offering for sin, he shall see his seed, he shall prolong his days, and the pleasure of the LORD shall prosper in his hand."-Isaiah 53:5, 10. The New Testament declared the heartbeat of the Kingdom's rule. "By one man's disobedience, the first Adam, many were made sinners. In fact, you and I were born sinners because of the first Adam's disobedience. Thank God, by one man's obedience, the second Adam, many of us were made righteous. For as by one man's disobedience many were made sinners, so by the obedience of one shall many be made righteous."-Romans 5:19. In 1968, God's grace and conviction came upon me, I repented and committed my life to Jesus as Lord and was born again. Today, grace gives me faith to believe and a will to obey. In our setbacks and sufferings, grace is being poured out on us to see the will of God, to be the will of God and to do the will.

History reports a Roman soldier who was facing pain and suffering. The commander told the soldier, "Your journey may be fatal." The soldier responded, "It is necessary for me to go, it is not necessary for me to live."

Sixth Positive Result Of The Storms Of Life:
Storms Coupled With Grace
Cause Us To Preserve And Mature

"Consider it pure joy, my brethren, whenever you face trials or storms of many kinds because you know the testing of your faith develops perseverance. Perseverance must finish its work so that you may become mature not lacking anything."-James 1:2. The scripture is clear; he who endures or perseveres to the end will be saved. It's not how we start the race; it is how we finish. Perseverance means to stay in the good fight of faith. The Apostle Paul was flogged, shipwrecked, persecuted, and imprisoned. Through it all, he said, "I have no regrets, I couldn't be more sure of my ground. The one I trusted in can take care of what He's trusted me to do right to the end."-II Timothy 1:12 (The Message).Jesus said, "To pray always and not faint."-Luke 18:1. To not faint means not to lose heart; not to give into doubt and discouragement. It means to endure, to persist, to persevere. Persistence, or perseverance, is a refusal to quit. A winner is not someone who never fails nor falls, but someone who never quits. This is a reality in all of our lives. There are times when quitting looks like the thing to do. In marriage, there is no perfect spouse. A time or two quitting may look good, but marriage is a covenant; it is for better or worse until death parts.

In the church world, there is not a perfect body or pastor. There is a time or two when quitting looks like the thing to do. Again, we are in covenant relationship. We endure through our differences and disagreements. We ride out the storms together. We endure and persevere through it all. We stay in the boat.

Persistence is a stubborn continuance in the midst of fierce opposition. "Nothing can take the place of persistence:

talent can't, intelligence can't, charisma can't. Thousands of men have talent, yet fail because they have not persisted or persevered," said President Teddy Roosevelt.

"So we have need of patience, endurance and perseverance, that after we have done the will of God we might receive the promise."-Hebrews 10:36. Endurance and perseverance, from God's inner strength, allow us to see the will of our Father and to do the will. Be patient, persevere, and be long-minded. We are in for the long haul. If the track of life is fast, we run. If the track is muddy and slow, we still run. We refuse to give in or to give up. One result of going through the storms of life coupled with grace is that we learn the power of perseverance or persistence. Our victory is always certain.

Seventh Positive Result Of The Storms Of Life:
Storms Test Our Faith In God's Word
And Faith Makes Impossible Things Happen

Again, in the midst of a hell-bending storm, Job stood and declared, "Though He slay me, yet I will trust Him."-Job 13:15. In the suffering of a horrendous storm, he lost 10 children, his wealth and his health. Yet, he held fast to his integrity and he remained faithful to the Lord, and in the end, experienced the seemingly impossible.

When you and I go through a major setback, we have a choice. We can grieve and regret until we die, or in the midst of tears, we can move forward. On October 31, 2006, I had a phone call from a church member. She called me crying and screaming that I needed to come to the hospital, they had pronounced her handsome 19-year-old son dead. A three-wheeler flipped on him, falling on his chest and crushing his physical heart. As a pastor, I walked through that tragic death and loss with her. In her tragic loss, the Holy Spirit gave me two *rhemas* to encourage her in the grace and faith of God: "While you are weeping, keep walking." "You are hurting, but by God's grace, you are healing." Two years later, following my oldest daughter's tragic death, these two *rhemas* became my confession. Pastors from all over the United States would call me and ask, "Rod, how are you doing?" My response, "I am weeping, but I am walking. I am hurting, but I am healing. And by God's grace, I am moving forward." My faith has been tested and proven through the storms of my family's life. Grace has done its deep work and we can proclaim with the Apostle Paul "as sorrowful, yet always rejoicing."-II Corinthians 6:10.

Chapter Four

Four Keys In Going Through Your Red Sea

It was a rough ride for the Aguillard clan from 2008 to 2011. We weathered three or four major storms. We went through several hard places and setbacks. At 72 years of age, I realize that it is all part of our earthy journey. There are two realities of the hard places in our life. The first is they are certain. We live in enemy territory and there are going to be demonic resistance and counter attacks. Secondly, the storms of life or hard places are necessary. It is our appointment to know and experience the indescribable grace of God.

In this chapter, we are going to a seemingly impossible

hard place called the Red Sea. The occasion and background is the deliverance of Israel from Egypt and the hand of Pharaoh, a type of the devil, and Egypt, a type of the world system.

The writer of Exodus describes the oppressor and our great deliverer. "And the LORD said, 'I have surely seen the affliction of my people which are in Egypt, and have heard their cry by reason of their taskmasters; for I know their sorrows; And I am come down to deliver them out of the hand of the Egyptians, and to bring them up out of that land unto a good land and a large, unto a land flowing with milk and honey; unto the place of the Canaanites, and the Hittites, and the Amorites, and the Perizzites, and the Hivites, and the Jebusites.'"-Exodus 3:7-8.

What He was then, He still is now. We serve a Heavenly Father who sees, who hears, who knows and who cares. Furthermore, we serve a God who delivers. He delivers us from the land of defeat and despair, a land of me-ism and materialism, a land of drugs and drink, a land of bondage and boredom, and a land of guilt and condemnation. Even more, He brings us into a good land, a land of promise and plenty, a land of peace and joy, a land of power and purpose. Yes, we have a great salvation; let's rejoice! Also, it is the land of the demonites, a land of opposition. Let's consider our opposition. Let's see a type of it by going to the Red Sea.

Exodus states that the children of Israel were encamped by the Red Sea, the "wilderness had shut them in."-Exodus 14:3. They were trapped in a hard place. This was a divine set-up because God had hardened the heart of Pharaoh to pursue the Israelites. He said, "I will harden Pharaoh's heart."-Exodus 14:1. God rules, not the devil. God brings us to a hard place on purpose for a purpose. "I will be honored upon Pharaoh."-Exodus 14:4. What Satan means for your destruction, God intends it for your edification. Our Father is not glorified in your suffering or hard place. He is glorified in your deliverance.

The normal response in our hard places is "to be sore afraid and to cry out."-Exodus 14:10. "The poor man crieth out and the Lord hears him and delivers him from all his troubles."-Psalms 34:6. The wrong response is the blame game. In their hard place, the Israelites blamed Moses for leading them into the place of wilderness of being shut in. In your hard place, don't blame mama or papa or grandmama or grandpapa. Don't blame your preacher or the school teacher, nor your spouse, who may be a louse. Please don't blame a crib trauma or a wicked mama. God is not dealing with the other players in your drama of life; He is dealing with you.

Allow the Holy Spirit to bring you to the end of your human efforts and give you the way of deliverance.

Here are four biblical words for your crossover through the hard places in your life.

First Crossover Word In Your Hard Place:
Fear Not

In their hard places "Moses said unto the people, fear ye not."-Exodus 14:13. In Exodus 15:1 and following, Abram faced family setbacks and certain wars. However, he had an upfront word, "Fear not, I am your shield and your exceeding great reward." In Chronicles 20:1 and following, King Jehosphat was surrounded by an overwhelming number of enemy nations. He was in a desperately hard place.

As he went low and cried out to the Lord, the spirit of the Lord came upon Jahazeil and he prophesied, "Be not afraid nor dismayed by reason of this great multitude because the battle is not yours, but Gods."-II Chronicles 20:15. King Jehosphat had an upfront word and in the end he won the day. As it has been said, God and one is a majority.

I was in a hard place in the Christmas season of 1991. I was one of the leaders in a pro-life movement called Rescue. Our mode of operation was to sit down in front of an abortion mill to shut it down for the day and to make a public statement that the murder of the innocent unborn children must stop. In doing so, we were guilty of criminal trespassing charges. Facing the judge, I refused to pay the fine and he sentenced me to one week in the Jefferson Parish jail during the Christmas week of 1991. The day my sentence began, they brought me to the second floor and as I entered the jail pod, I sensed an ominous spirit. My cell mate was "Lizard." I asked him, "Who is in here?" He began to describe my fellow prisoners: one murdered his wife; another beat a grandmother to death with a bat; another had 75 counts of child molestation; and Lizard was in for car theft. The judge was supposed to have assigned me into the prison area for those who had committed misdemeanors. Instead, he incarcerated me with the serious felons.

In my hard place, I began to fear, but the day before, God had given me an upfront promise: "The perfect love of God will cast out all fear." On Christmas Eve, I had the joy and privilege to preach to 17 hopeless felons. My text was, "But when the fullness of the time was come, God sent forth his Son, made of a woman, made under the law, to redeem them that were under the law, that we might receive the adoption of sons."-Galatians 4:4-5. Following the message, I got to pray a sinner's prayer with the child molester. Later in the day, I sat in a corner with a young man indicted for raping and killing a nine-year-old girl and then burying her in leaves. I had the joy of leading him in a sinner's prayer.

What the judge meant for evil, God turned it for good. He brought me into a hard place on purpose for a purpose. The Christmas week was the best Christmas season of my whole life. God is good, God rules and God has the last word in your hard place, if you will trust Him. Fear not!

Second Crossover Word In Your Hard Place: Stand Still

"Stand still and see the salvation of the Lord."-Exodus 14:13. Stand still. The Apostle Paul also gave us this delivering word for our hard place. He said, "Take on the whole armor of God that you may be able to withstand in the evil day (the hard place) and having done all, Stand!"-Ephesians 6:11. Some of you would say today, "I have done it all! I have prayed, I have fasted, I have stood on the promises, and I have confessed the promises, but I still have no breakthrough. What do I do now?" Stand! Having done all, just stand.

In my personal hard place of 1988, I became involved in the Rescue Movement, going to the abortion mills for the life of the unborn. All hell broke loose. The enemy counterattacked my home, my family, and my ministry. My mother-in-law was in a nervous breakdown; my oldest daughter had her first breakdown and was in a mental ward; my oldest son left his wife for another woman; and other pressures came against the church body. I was in a heartbroken and hard place. One Sunday morning, standing on the platform of our church during a celebration service, tears in my eyes and a tear in my heart, I stood flat footed and made a decision. I said, "Lord Jesus I am going to serve you and praise you. It doesn't matter what it looks like or feels like." At the heartfelt decision just to stand, the grace of God kicked in and I began to move forward in victory. The great good news in your hard place: God is not a respecter of persons. He is rich unto all who call. As you stand in your hard place, Pharaoh behind and the Red Sea in front of you, stand without murmuring and give thanks. Stand still and shout through your storms. Get ready. Your Red Sea is about to open. God Himself delights, not in your hard place. He delights in your deliverance. Rejoice!

Third Crossover Word In Your Hard Place: Hold Your Peace

"The Lord shall fight for you, and ye shall hold your peace."-Exodus 14:14. Refuse to speak the evil report of unbelief or doubt. Our Lord Jesus said it well, "Don't doubt in your heart (refuse it), but believe those things which you saith shall come to pass. You shall have whatsoever you said."-Mark 11:23. See it! Seize it! Say it! And keep on saying it and you will have it, deliverance from your hard place. Don't be foolish with super faith. That is, don't deny your setback or heartbreak, but simply declare Him. Don't deny your financial hard place, but as a tither, declare Him as your Jehovah Jireh, the Lord your provider. Your lack is an opportunity for His provision if you will declare and trust Him. Don't deny your physical sickness; it is real. Rather, declare Him as your Jehovah Rapha, He is the Lord your healer! He bore your sickness and took your pains. He was made sick with your sickness so that you would be made whole with His health and healing. Your sickness is an opportunity for His healing, declare Him and trust Him!

Hold your peace. Refuse to complain and to murmur. You can do it. Rather, in everything give thanks for this is the will of your Father in Heaven. This is a truth, "Our light affliction is but for a moment, it is working for us an eternal work of glory."-II Corinthians 4:17. It is true, all things are indeed working for our good: bad things, good things, sad things, and glad things. As I wrote earlier, God will have the last word on everything, if you will just simply trust Him.

Fear not. Stand still and hold your peace.

Hold your peace. Don't charge the body. In spite of her flaws and faults, she is still God's girl, His Bride. My last three children were born just a year or so apart. Together, they were a handful for their mother to raise at home during the day. At certain times, when I arrived home late into the afternoon, they had exhausted their mama. I would confront them on their behavior and on occasion said, "Stop it! That's my wife you are messing with." Needless, to say, the fear of God would come upon them. Therefore, don't accuse the body. Don't sow discord. Hold your peace. At times, my wife is slow to respond to a setback. However, in a major crisis or hard place, she is a sure source of comfort and strength. On December 11, 2008, during the season of our oldest daughter's tragic death, God's people came to our side. They kissed us, hugged us, loved us, and cared for us. For days, spiritual sons and daughters slept in our home just to be with us as a source of comfort. The body of Christ is the greatest organism of strength on the planet.

Hold your peace. Don't charge God. In Job 2:3, the Lord challenged Satan that even in the midst of Job's setbacks he held fast his integrity, he refused to charge God. Follow Job's example, don't charge God and at some point in your hard place, you will have Job's results: The deliverer will restore and compensate for all your loss and your latter end will be greater than your former end.

Fourth Crossover Word In Your Hard Place: Go Forward

"And the LORD said unto Moses, Wherefore criest thou unto me? Speak unto the children of Israel, that they go forward."-Exodus 14:15. The Lord challenged Moses, "Why criest?" There is a time to cry, the poor man crieth out and the Lord hears him."-Psalms 34:6. But, there is a time to stop crying out. There is a time to get up and move forward. Another translation states, "Wherefore should thou press your petitions any further, it is granted. Now get up and go forward."-Exodus 14:15. Yes, there is a time to get up, get over it and move on. You can't fix your past. You have no grace to live in the past. You have no grace to unscramble the eggs of your past; relive your first marriage; undo your mistakes; or correct the sin of your youth. You have no grace to live in the tomorrows, either. Plan well, but don't try to live tomorrow, today. You have grace for the day, and you have grace to cry out, to get up and to move forward. Forgive others for what they have done to you, forgive yourself, and realize that the Father has forgiven you and gives you grace to move forward. Just do it!

Moses was still opposed. Pharaoh was still behind him and the Red Sea was still before him. He was still shut in the wilderness and still in a hard place, yet God said to "move forward."

You may be knocked down because of your hard place, but you can't stay down. I have been knocked down, but never knocked out. Over my 44 years of serving Him, I have been knocked down a hundred times to the count of eight. But, near that count of 10, something called the indescribable grace of God kicks in and I am in victory for another day. If you don't get up, if you go on a pity party in your hard place, the devil will knock your head off and steal your praise.

But, as you fear not, as you hold your peace as you get up and go forward, the Lord Himself will fight for you. Read the report, "And it came to pass in the morning watch, the Lord locked down and troubled the enemy."-Exodus 14:24. One look from Heaven and it throws confusion into the ranks of our ancient enemy. "Let God arise and let His enemies be scattered."-Psalms 68:1. Israel is no match for Pharaoh and his armies. But, at the same time, Pharaoh's armies are no match for God. You are no match for the darkness that opposes you, but your enemy or hard place is no match for the Lord Himself. He has dominion. He has all authority in heaven and earth. Just one look or one word from Him and our enemy is scattered.

The deliverance goes on. "He took off their chariot wheels."-Exodus 14:25. Today, tomorrow, and next week, the Holy Spirit has the authority and power to take the wheels off your adversary. Then, the response of our opposition comes: "Let us flee for the Lord fights for them."-Exodus 14:25. So today, in your hard place or in your difficulty: 1. Fear not: submit unto God and resist the devil. 2. Stand still: refuse to give up or give in. Stand on the promises! 3. Hold your peace! Refuse to speak an evil report of doubt. Refuse to charge God. Refuse to charge the Body of Christ. 4. Get up and go forward. Your Red Sea will open. Your victory is certain.

Chapter Five

In Your Personal Storms Or Hard Place: Trust Him

In Asia, we had the sentence of death on us, that we should not trust in ourselves, but in God who raiseth the dead. In whom we trust that, He will yet deliver us."-II Corinthians 1:8-11. The bedrock of real faith in delivering us from the storms of life is to trust Him. All of us have too much self-will, so the Holy Spirit is using the setback and sorrows to put the sentence of death in us that we will not trust in our self effort but in Him. Let's trust Him. I remind you that we serve, "the Father of mercies."-II Corinthians 1:3. He is not stingy with mercy and he does not have limited mercies. "Thy truth is unto the clouds; thy mercy is great unto the Heavens."-Psalms 57:9. God is merciful. He is ready to forgive, He is ready to deliver, and He is ready to restore us. "His mercies are new every morning, great is His faithfulness."-Lamentations 3:23. Every morning, I sit at the feet of Jesus and receive from the mercy seat of our Heavenly Father.

Let's trust Him. "He is the God of all comfort!"-II Corinthians 1:3. The Holy Spirit is our Great Comforter. He is alongside us to strengthen us through the storms of life. He is our inside Strengthener. In the midst of a personal storm, when your human strength gives out, His strength will kick in. During a time period in the middle 1980s, I was in the valley of discouragement. I was hoping that Jesus would come back that night and rescue me. Have you ever been there? You might be there now or it may come soon. As I went to bed, my victory was lost and all hope seemed gone. In the midnight hour of my soul, the Holy Spirit visited me with a vision in the night. I saw myself on a narrow path in the middle of a dark forest. I was walking against a blizzard with snow to my knees. This is a Cajun nightmare! In my distress and weary journey, I simply fell in the snow to die a slow death. In the vision, my oldest daughter, lovely Lynne, came and knelt by me with her hands folded and began to pray for my strength. That morning, when I awoke, my spirit was full of joy, and my mind and body were full of strength. Indeed, the Comforter had come through a vision of the night.

Let's trust Him. He is the God of Hope, the God of a better day. "Now the God of hope fill you with all joy and peace in believing."-Romans 15:13. I have hope. I have a confident expectation that God Himself is working all things for my good, even the bad and sad things. There may be weeping for the night, but joy comes in the morning. I am confident that He is storing your tears in a bottle and recording your tears in a book, and the very day you call for help, the tide of your battle turns.

Let's trust Him. "Trust in the Lord with all your heart, lean not to your own understanding."-Proverbs 3:5. Trust means to be secure in. It means to serve Him regardless of the outcome. It means to acknowledge before the world that God will have the last word, not the devil or your negative circumstances. In the spring of 1988, Mary and I were having a gray morning. We were driving to Oschner Clinic in New Orleans where our oldest daughter was confined to a mental ward. Our hearts were broken. On the way to Oschner's, we were listening to a Dr. Dobson special on the radio playing a message by E.V. Hill at his wife's funeral. In the crisis of her condition, he went to the hospital chapel and prayed for healing and recovery. The Holy Spirit spoke to him, "Whether she lives or dies, just trust me." We wept as we embraced that word for our daughter's deliverance from a mental nightmare, "Just trust me."

I am going to share with you five statements of trust to embrace as you go through the storms of life. The five statements of trust are recorded in Psalms 37:3-7.

First Statement Of Trust

"Trust in the Lord and do good; so shalt thou dwell in the land, and verily be fed."-Psalms 37:3. Trust means to entrust, to let another be in charge. Trust is the place of no struggling or striving at the oars. It is an act of faith and surrender that declares that God is in charge. In August 1988, I was traveling to Atlanta to join a movement called Rescue to stand against the murder of unborn babies. I was apprehensive because I knew the strategy was to sit down in front of an abortion mill and be hauled away in paddy wagons to prison. As I traveled, the Holy Spirit came to me and spoke three *rhemas*: "You are a sheep led to the slaughter." I didn't like this word even though rescue was a position of humility, not violent resistance. Secondly, He said to me, "You are not in the devil's hands, you are in God's hands." That was a great word of comfort that invoked inner faith and trust. Thank God that the devil doesn't rule. If he ruled, all of us would be dead by morning. All of us are in the Father's hand and He will sustain us through the storms and deliver us in due season. Thirdly, the word that came to me and that stills lives in me was, "You have grace for the day." Again, we don't have grace to live in the past. We cannot change what has already happened. Our past will not determine our future. His daily presence will determine our tomorrows. We have no grace to live tomorrow. Jesus said take no thought for tomorrow. Don't worry about tomorrow,, there is enough evil in today. As I was incarcerated for trying to save the lives of the unborn, I had grace to live through that day. As I have gone through some horrific setbacks and sorrows, I have had grace to live one day at a time. I repeat: His grace is sufficient. By His grace through faith, I am going to trust Him through it all. Jesus is Lord. He is in charge and we can trust Him for a victorious outcome.

Second Statement Of Trust

"Delight thyself also in the Lord and He shall give thee the desires of my heart."-Psalms 37:4. Delight means to have great joy and pleasure in waiting on God. It means to bask in His word and in His presence. I spent Christmas Day of 2011 at home enjoying my family, food, fun and fellowship. I delighted in them and in that day. The day after, on December 26, 2011, I spend that day alone with the Lord and delighted in His fellowship. Out of that fellowship, I wrote many of the thoughts in this chapter.

Years ago, Pastor Larry Lea shared the three D's of communion for maturity: **Desire** – The Holy Spirit creates a hunger for God's Word and God's presence; **Discipline** – We must set a quiet time and a quite place to seek and to be still and know God. I choose the early mornings, right at daybreak. I sit in a cozy corner of my living room to wait on the Lord. **Delight** – Following desire and discipline, delight comes. As a waiter, I am addicted to sit at the feet of Jesus by morning. Most of my ministry is born at the feet of Jesus. It is at His feet, you will experience divine osmosis, absorbing the presence of God. In His presence, there is fullness of joy, and the bedrock of trust and faith is laid in your heart.

Third Statement Of Trust

"Commit thy way unto the Lord, trust also in Him and He shall bring it to pass."-Psalms 37:5. Commit means to roll it on the Lord. Don't be a mule and try to carry all your burdens and the burdens of others; roll it on the Lord. Commit and roll your straying spouse onto the Lord. Commit and roll your wayward child or children onto the Lord. You can't change them; only God can. Commit and roll the financial lack of your job or your business onto the Lord. Commit and roll your worries and fears onto the Lord. By morning, by day and by night, keep rolling the problems and pressures onto Him. A word of wisdom, "Commit your works unto the Lord, (that is take God into partnership in whatever you do) and every thought and plan will be established."-Proverbs 16:3. We have been trained in so much humanism and self effort that trusting Him and committing it all to Him does not come easy. By day, we have to submit our hearts to Him and allow the Holy Spirit to renew our minds. Help us, dear Jesus!

King Solomon, in his grandest hour, was just made king over Israel. He made this statement of surrendered trust, saying, "I am but a little child. I do not know how to go out or come in, give me wisdom to judge your people."-I Kings 3:7. In his humility, as he rolled it onto the Lord, God made him the wisest man who ever lived. From now through the rest of your days, roll it on the Lord and then He shall bring forth thy righteousness as the light of the noon day.

Fourth Statement Of Trust

"Rest in the Lord and wait patiently for Him."-Psalms

37:7. Stop all your smart ways and self-effort. God is smarter than you. He can fix it in you. Often, too often, I have become a Jacob, trying to work things out in my own flesh and self-effort. I am not stupid, but I do at least seven stupid things a week. I am learning to rest in the Lord, to be still, to slow down, and smell the roses. Help me, dear Jesus. Rest means to trust Him, to let go and let God, to let the offense go, to let the hurt go, to forgive, and just trust God for the outcome. He will vindicate righteousness. He will win the day for you; just trust Him. "Who, when he was reviled, reviled not again; when he suffered, he threatened not; but committed himself to him that judgeth righteously."-I Peter 2:23. Rest means sweet surrender. That's not easy for most of us trained in self-will rather than God's will. Rest and just yoke up with our Lord Jesus. He said, "Come unto me, all ye that labor and are heavy laden and I will give you rest. Yoke up with me and ye shall find rest unto your souls."-Matthew 11:28-29. Let's do it!

Fifth Statement Of Trust

"Though He slay me, yet will I trust Him."-Job 15:13. In my understanding, this is the highest statement of faith and surrender in the entire Bible. This great statement of faith means that when everything is against me, I will declare that all things are working for my good. It means I will proceed in His purposes even though it might cost all that is dear to me. Dr. Hudson Taylor, who brought Jesus to inland China during his lifetime, prematurely lost his wife and two children to death on the mission field. At that time, he stated that his grief was unbearable, yet he went forward in the purposes of God and the God of all comfort visited him in the midnight hours to strengthen him. Following our oldest daughter's untimely and tragic death, we suffered grief that was almost unbearable. But, in the midst of our darkest hours, we worshipped Him and made a decision to move forward in God's purpose. Two weeks following Christmas of 2008, we were back in the field pastoring pastors.

Though he slay me, yet will I trust Him, means when worst comes to worst, I will still praise Him and serve Him. The trusting psalmist declared, "My heart is fixed, I will sing and give praise."-Psalms 57:7. Again, I refer to probably the most trusting person in all of scripture. Job, who lost it all to the demonic attacks of the darkness. He lost his children, and his wealth, and he expressed his grief openly, "He arose and tore his robe and shaved his head."-Job 1:20. But then, he fell to the ground. When worst came to worst, he worshiped God, "The Lord gave and the Lord has taken away, blessed be the name of the Lord."-Job 1:21. As we face our storms, let's trust Him.

Let's rise up and bless Him regardless of what seems to be the outcome. In due season, He will deliver us and in our deliverance, we will glorify Him. "Father, in Jesus name, we will not lean to our stinking thinking and our self-effort. Rather, we will bow and bend at the throne of grace in surrendered trust. We will receive mercy in our time of need and we will be more than overcomers in this life. "For yours is the Kingdom and the power and the glory forever. Amen!"-Matthew 6:13.

Need additional copies?

To order more copies of

Going Through The **Storms of Life**

contact NewBookPublishing.com

- ❐ Order online at:

  NewBookPublishing.com/Bookstore

- ❐ Call 877-311-5100 or

- ❐ Email Info@NewBookPublishing.com

Call for multiple copy discounts!